Celebrate (Kindergarten)

Written by Marcia Noel Hornok

Illustrated by Susan Hendron

Cover Illustrated by Kathryn Marlin

"... We do not make requests of you because we are righteous, but because of your great mercy."
(Daniel 9:18)

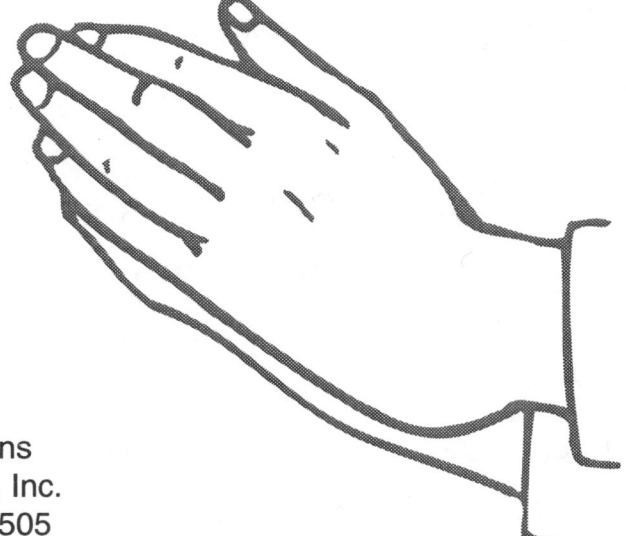

All rights reserved—Printed in the U.S.A.
Copyright © 1999 Shining Star Publications
A Division of Frank Schaffer Publications, Inc.
23740 Hawthorne Blvd., Torrance, CA 90505

Notice! Pages may be reproduced for home or classroom use only, not for commercial resale. No part of this publication may be reproduced for storage in a retrieval system, or transmitted in any form or by any means—electronic, mechanical, recording, etc.—without the prior written permission of the publisher. Reproduction of these materials for an entire school or school system is strictly prohibited.

Unless otherwise indicated, the New International Version of the Bible was used in preparing the activities in this book. Scripture taken from the HOLY BIBLE, NEW INTERNATIONAL VERSION. Copyright © 1973, 1978, 1984 International Bible Society. Used by permission of Zondervan Bible Publishers.

Table of Contents

To Parents and Teachers 3
Keep Your Heart in Tune (Craft) 4
Jesus Prays for Me (Finger Play) 5
Jesus Taught About Prayer
 (Action Verse) 6
Could I Please Have . . . ? 7
Praying Like Jesus 8
Read the Bible 9
God Answers (Bulletin Board) 10
Trust God's Answers 11
Reasons to Pray 12
Splash Into Bible Truths 13
What Is God Like? 14
Comparing Our Fathers (Game) 15
"God's Good Gifts" Can (Craft) 16
Prayer Calendar (Bulletin Board) 17
Alphabetical Order Praise Cards 18
Loving and Praising God (Songs) 19
Kitchen Orchestra 20
Sing Praise to God (Songs) 21–22
Magical Musical Sounds
 (Finger Play) 23
Thanksgiving Place Mat 24
"Express Your Emotions" Book 25
I'm Wonderfully Made 26
Pray Banner 27
Special Things to Pray for
 (Bulletin Board and Activity) ... 28–29
Egg Request (Game) 30
A Gift of Love 31
Prayer Puzzle 32
Pray Throughout the Day
 (Action Story) 33–34
Prayer Grid (Game) 35
Praying People Puzzles 36
Lots of People Prayed 37
Daniel Prayed No Matter What! 38
Be Like Daniel 39
Happy or Sad? 40
Wanna-Be Song 41
Any Place, Any Time 42
Pray and Be Happy! 43
Prayer Fun (Action Verses) 44
Special Cards 45
Let's Go Pray! 46
Rhyme Time 47
Sssh! Prayer in Progress
 (Door Hanger) 48

 # To Parents and Teachers

What a fun way for children to learn all about the power of prayer! This book is packed with a wonderful variety of activities the children can complete to help them learn about Bible people who prayed, who and what to pray for, when and where to pray, why and how to pray, and much more.

Activities featured include crafts, songs, finger plays, action Bible verses, mazes, and puzzles, among many others. And not only will these activities help the children learn about prayer, but they will also help them practice and improve such skills as following directions, comparing and contrasting, critical thinking, discussing, coloring, and drawing.

Each activity features at least one Bible verse relating to prayer. Be sure to discuss these with the children and their relevance to the children's lives. You might also encourage the children to memorize as many of these verses as possible.

You will love watching your children have a wonderful time learning all about prayer and the valuable role it can play in our lives!

..."Lord, teach us to pray..." Luke 11:1

Keep Your Heart in Tune

Craft

. . . Sing and make music in your heart to the Lord, always giving thanks to God the Father for everything . . . (Ephesians 5:19–20)

This craft is a perfect way to remind children to pray.

Materials Needed (per child):
one copy of the pattern to the right, glue, four 6"-pieces of yarn or string, scissors

Directions:
1. Give each child a copy of the ukelele pattern.
2. Have the children cut out their ukeleles.
3. Help the children run a line of glue on each line.
4. Then they can attach the yarn or string pieces on top of the glue.

Discuss with the children how we "keep in tune" with God by praying every time we think about it, by singing songs in our minds or out loud, and by thanking God for everything.

This could also be a bulletin board display by making one large ukelele or guitar. Add this title: *Praying Keeps Your Heart in Tune With God.* You could hang the children's ukeleles around it.

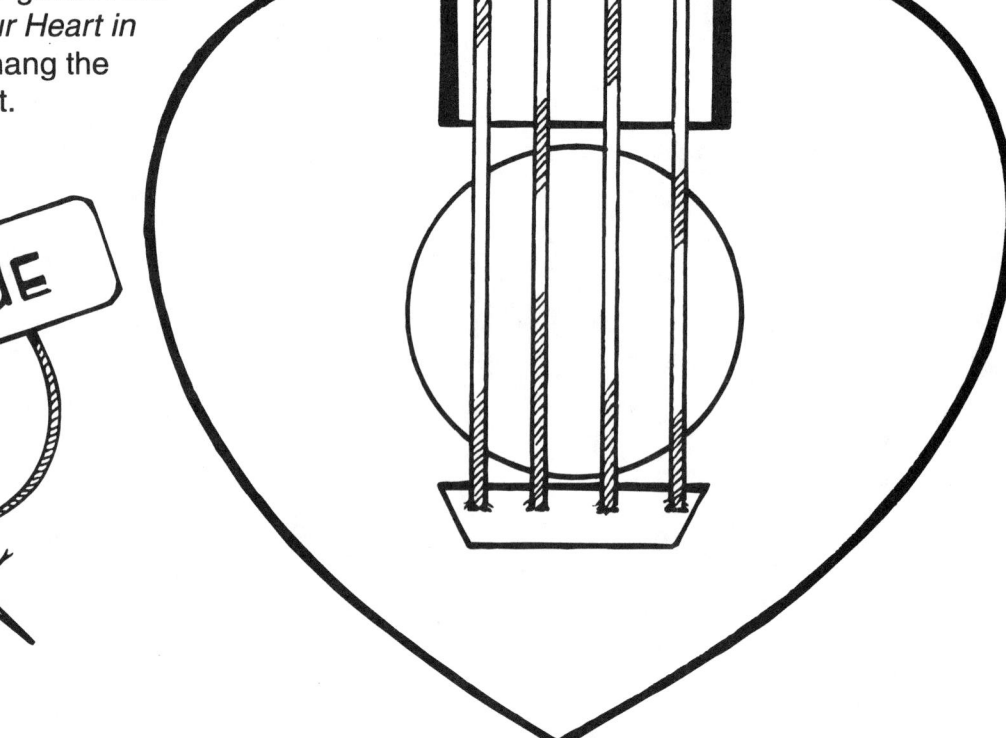

© Shining Star Publications

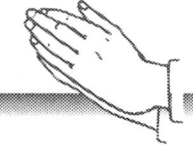

Jesus Prays for Me

Finger Play

"... I pray also for those who will believe in me through their message, that all of them may be one, Father, just as you are in me and I am in you ..." (John 17:20–21)

The finger play below is fun for the children to do to help them learn that Jesus prays for them.

Materials Needed:
a musical instrument such as a guitar or piano

Directions:
Play discordant chords on the instrument. Ask the children how it sounds and why. Then play some harmonious chords. Ask the children how it sounds. Explain to the children that when we do something that is not nice, it is like being out of tune. When we obey God's laws, we are "in tune" with God. Then teach the children the finger play below.

God remembers me.	(Point up. Point to forehead. Point to self.)
God remembers me.	(Point up. Point to forehead. Point to self.)
I am written on His hand.	(Write on one palm with your finger.)
God remembers me.	(Point up. Point to forehead. Point to self.)
Jesus prays for me.	(Point up. Fold hands like praying. Point to self.)
Jesus prays for me.	(Point up. Fold hands like praying. Point to self.)
With the nail prints in His hands,	(Point to center of each palm.)
Jesus prays for me.	(Point up. Fold hands like praying. Point to self.)
The Spirit prays for me.	(Fold hands like praying. Point to self.)
The Spirit prays for me.	(Fold hands like praying. Point to self.)
He is living in my heart.	(Use index fingers to trace a heart outline on chest.)
And He prays for me.	(Fold hands like praying. Point to self.)

Jesus Taught About Prayer

Action Verse

"Ask and it will be given to you; seek and you will find; knock and the door will be opened to you. For everyone who asks receives; he who seeks finds; and to him who knocks, the door will be opened." (Matthew 7:7–8)

The children will learn what Jesus taught about prayer by doing the action verse below. To help the children memorize these verses, teach them the motions below. Keep the motions smooth, making them flow from one movement to the next.

"Ask	(Fold hands like praying.)
and it will be given to you;	(Move hands forward from waistline, palms up.)
seek	(Form a "C" with one hand and hold it up to eye; move it in small circles.)
and you will find;	(Pretend to pick up something.)
knock	(Make knocking motion.)
and the door will be opened to you.	(Start with hands together and spread arms wide, to the side.)
For everyone who asks	(Fold hands like praying.)
receives;	(Hold hands out like receiving something.)
he who seeks	(Form a "C" with one hand and hold it up to eye; move it in small circles.)
finds;	(Pretend to pick up something.)
and to him who knocks,	(Make knocking motion.)
the door will be opened."	(Start with hands together and spread arms wide, to the side.)

Could I Please Have . . . ?

"Ask and it will be given to you . . ." (Matthew 7:7)

Praying to God often means asking Him for something. Jesus tells us that if we ask for something, we will get it.

Circle the things a dad would give his child if the child asked for them. Draw an X on things the father would probably not give his child.

Praying Like Jesus

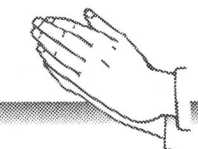

"Father, if you are willing, take this cup from me; yet not my will, but yours be done." (Luke 22:42)

The song below will help remind children that Jesus prayed and that we need to pray just like He did. Talk to the children about how Jesus prayed in Gethsemane (Matthew 26:36–46) and about doing what God wants us to do even when it is hard. Then teach them the song below.

What Jesus Prayed
(Tune: "Mary Had a Little Lamb")

In the garden, Jesus prayed,
Jesus prayed, Jesus prayed.
In the garden, Jesus prayed,
And this is what He said:

"Not my will but Yours be done,
Yours be done, Yours be done.
Not my will but Yours be done."
Yes, that's what Jesus prayed.

I will pray what Jesus prayed,
Jesus prayed, Jesus prayed.
I will pray what Jesus prayed,
And this is what I'll say:

"Not my will but Yours be done,
Yours be done, Yours be done.
Not my will but Yours be done,
In Jesus' name, Amen."

Prayer Endings

Christians generally close their prayers as follows: "in Jesus' name, Amen." This practice is based on verses that teach us to pray in Jesus' name, such as John 14:13–14, 26; 15:16; 16:23–26.

To end a prayer time, have the children sing the words below.

Yours is the kingdom;

Yours is the power;

Yours is the glory;

Forevermore, Amen.

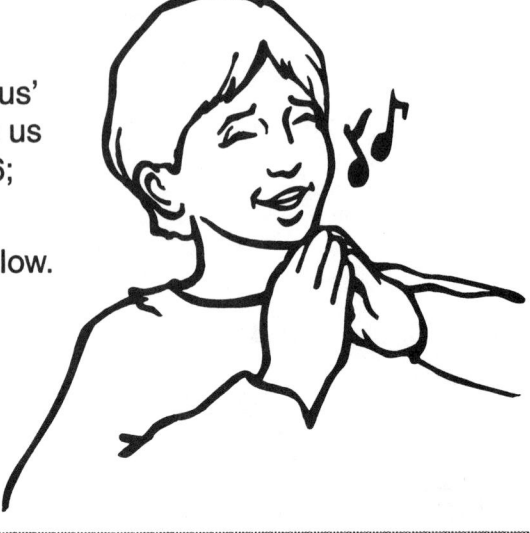

© Shining Star Publications

SS48832

Read the Bible

Let the word of Christ dwell in you . . . (Colossians 3:16)

Many people use the Bible to pray. Find the 5 hidden Bibles. Color them red. Color the rest of the picture. Trace the words.

Read the Bible!

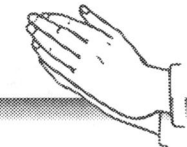

God Answers
Bulletin Board

This is the confidence we have in approaching God: that if we ask anything according to his will, he hears us. (1 John 5:14)

This bulletin board provides the perfect way for the children to see how God answers prayers.

Materials Needed:
black, red, yellow, and green paper; scissors; push pins; sticky notes or 2" x 3" cards; black marker; stapler

Directions:
Divide the bulletin board into three horizontal sections. Put green paper on top, yellow in the middle, and red on the bottom. The yellow section can be slightly larger than the other two because this section will hold the most prayer requests.

Staple a black strip of paper vertically down the middle of the board. Staple three equal-sized circles—one green, one yellow, and one red—to this strip.

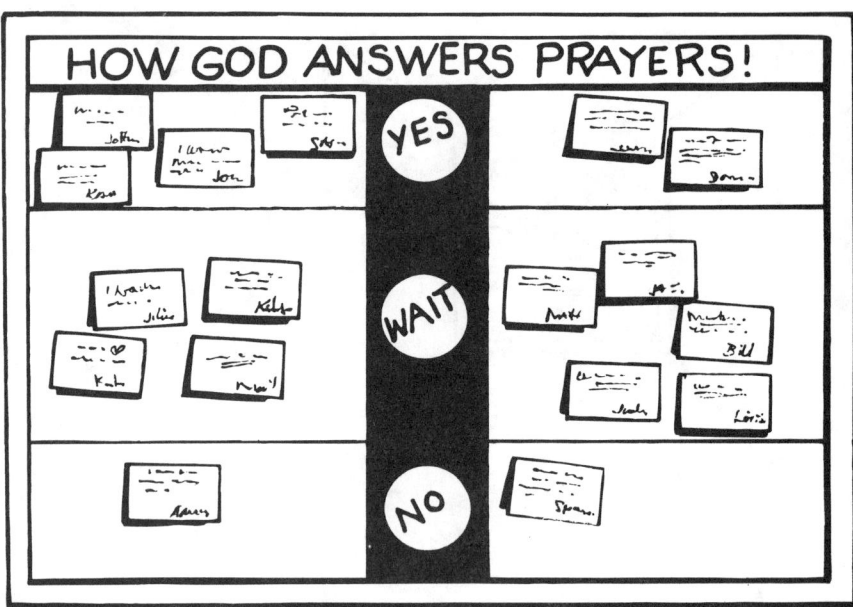

Use a marker to write "Yes" in the green circle, "Wait" in the yellow circle, and "No" in the red circle.

Ask children what their prayer requests are. Write each request on a separate sticky note or card, along with the child's name. Place these on the yellow strip. Then pray for each request. Depending on the ability of the children, perhaps you could assign the requests to them. Let them repeat a prayer after you, if needed.

Regularly review the requests to see if God has answered "Yes" or "No." If so, move the request to the green or red section. If not, pray for that request again. Add other requests as the children present them.

Biblical examples of God answering prayers these three ways:
Hannah prayed for a son. God answered "Yes." (1 Samuel 1:27)

Paul prayed for removal of a thorn in his flesh. God answered "No." (2 Corinthians 12:7–9)

David prayed for deliverance from his enemies. God answered "Wait." (Psalm 13:1–2, 22:2, 27:14)

Trust God's Answers

"'Call to me and I will answer you and tell you great and unsearchable things you do not know.'" (Jeremiah 33:3)

Help the children understand that God has reasons for the answers He gives us to our prayers. Then teach them the songs below to remind them of this.

God Answers
(Tune: chorus of "Battle Hymn of the Republic")

I will pray, and God will answer. *(Repeat two more times.)*
Sometimes He answers, "Yes."

I will pray, and God will answer. *(Repeat two more times.)*
Sometimes He answers, "No."

I will pray, and God will answer. *(Repeat two more times.)*
Sometimes He answers, "Wait."

Who Answers Our Prayers?

Teach the children their lines and sing this song together to the tune of "Twinkle, Twinkle, Little Star."

Teacher: Who will hear and answer our prayers?
Children: God will hear and answer our prayers.
All: Sometimes God will answer "Yes."
He is good and knows what's best.
Teacher: Who will hear and answer our prayers?
Children: God will hear and answer our prayers.

Teacher: Who will hear and answer our prayers?
Children: God will hear and answer our prayers.
All: Sometimes God will answer "No."
He wants us to learn and grow.
Teacher: Who will hear and answer our prayers?
Children: God will hear and answer our prayers.

Teacher: Who will hear and answer our prayers?
Children: God will hear and answer our prayers.
All: Sometimes God will answer "Wait."
He is wise and oh so great.
Teacher: Who will hear and answer our prayers?
Children: God will hear and answer our prayers.

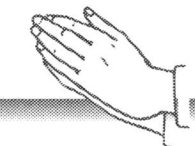

Reasons to Pray

Let us then approach the throne of grace with confidence, so that we may receive mercy and find grace to help us in our time of need. (Hebrews 4:16)

There are many reasons why we should pray—for someone, for something, to say "I'm sorry," etc. Discuss these and other reasons with the children. Then teach them the song below.

When I Pray
(Tune: "Are You Sleeping?")

This song can be done as an echo song with the children repeating you.

God will hear me,
When I pray.
He will answer wisely,
When I pray.

I am sorry,
For my sins.
I know You forgive me.
Thank You, Lord.

God will help me,
When I pray.
He will make me stronger,
When I pray.

I obey God,
When I pray.
I show how I love Him,
When I pray.

How God Talks to Us

. . . the Lord our God is near us whenever we pray to him. (Deuteronomy 4:7)

Discuss friendship with the children. Explain that if they never talked to their best friend, and their best friend never talked to them, they really wouldn't have a very good friendship. Tell the children that we talk to God by praying, and He talks to us when we read or hear His Word, the Bible. This type of communication is essential to our spiritual growth and walk with God.

Teach the children the finger play below to help them better understand how God talks to us.

I <u>talk</u> to God through <u>prayer</u>.
God <u>listens</u> to my <u>prayers</u>.
God <u>talks</u> to me through the <u>Bible</u>.
I <u>listen</u> to the <u>Bible</u>.

(TALK(S)—Cup hands around mouth.)
(PRAYER(S)—Fold hands as if praying.)
(LISTEN(S)—Cup hands around ears.)
(BIBLE—Open and close hands like a book.)

Splash Into Bible Truths

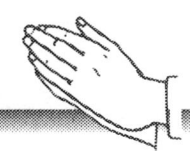

Copy the letters from the water slide in order onto the spaces under the slide. Read the message from Jesus to us.

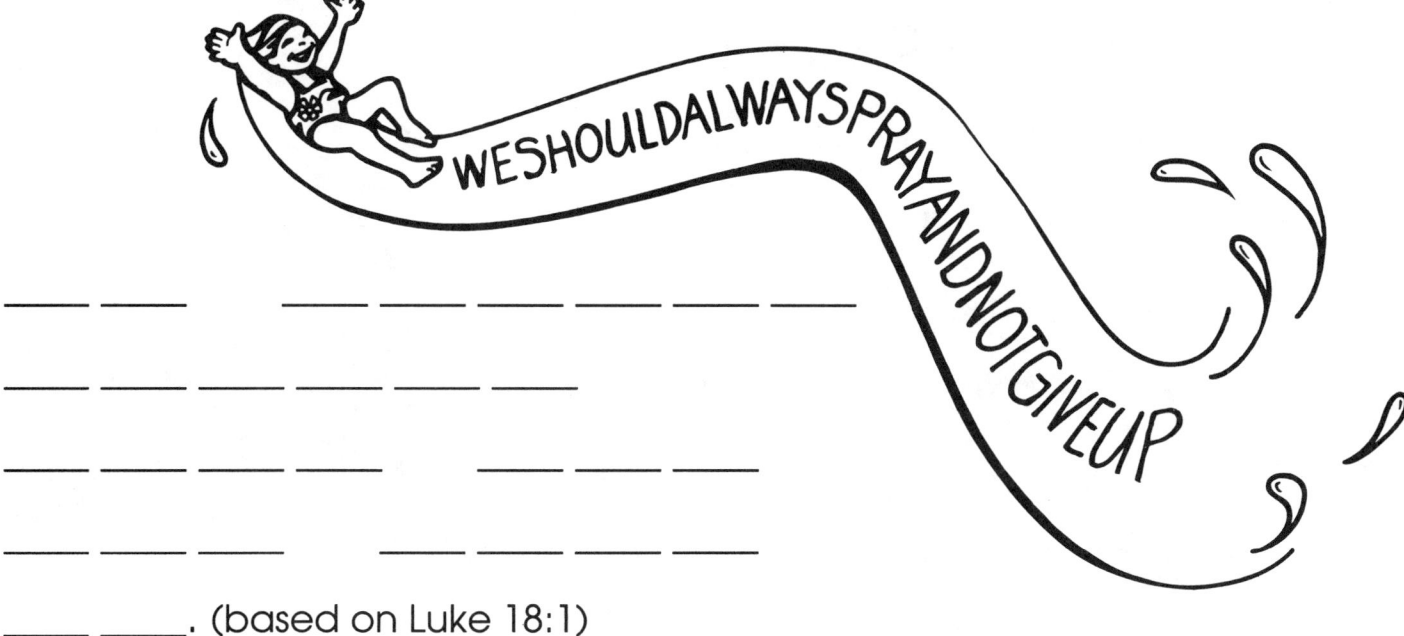

___ _____

_____

_____

_____

___ ___. (based on Luke 18:1)

Copy the letters from the water slide below in order onto the spaces. Read the Bible promise about prayer.

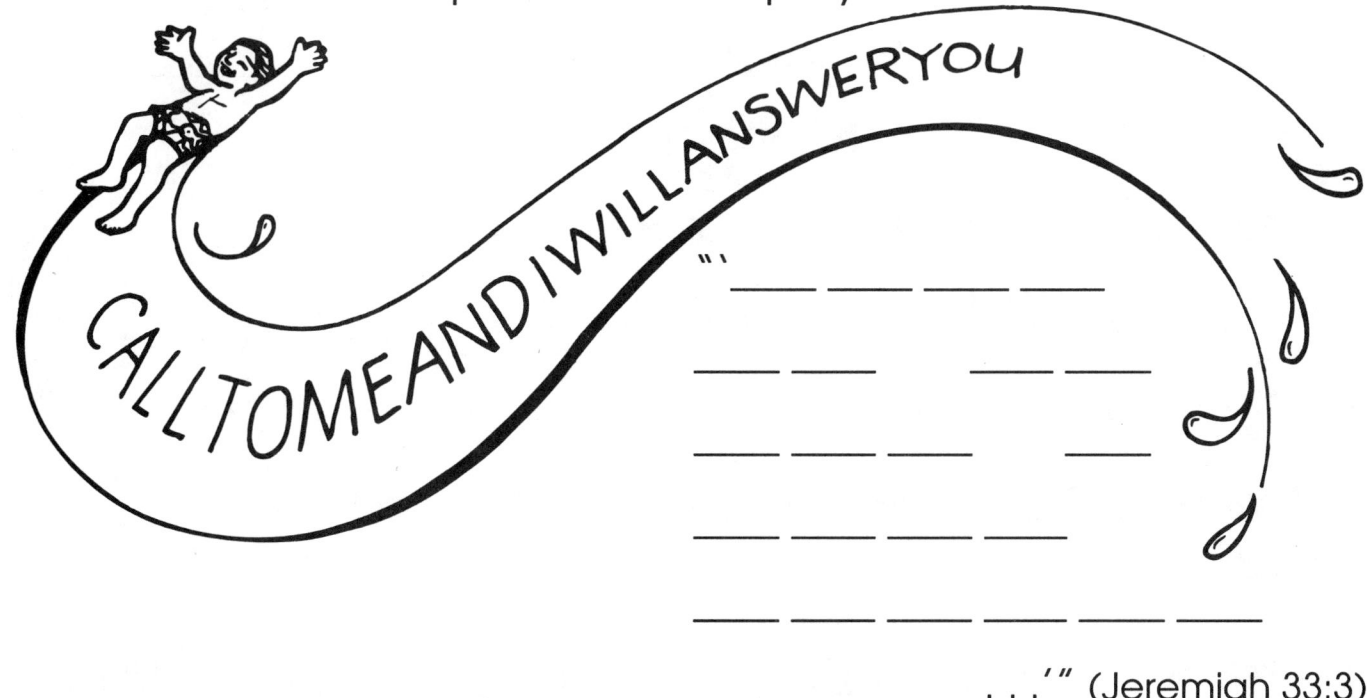

"_____

___ __

____

_____

___ ___ ___ . . .'" (Jeremiah 33:3)

What Is God Like?

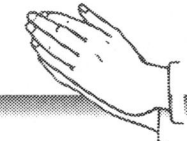

The Lord is near to all who call on him, to all who call on him in truth. (Psalm 145:18)

Copy each capitalized word in each sentence into the blank.

1. Because God is GOOD, He gives _____ gifts.

2. Because God is LOVE, He _____S me.

3. Because God MADE everything, He _____ me.

4. Because God KNOWS everything, He _____ all about me.

5. Because God is everywHERE, He is _____ with me.

6. Because God is RIGHTeous, everything He does is _____.

7. Because God KEEPS His word, He always _____ His promises.

8. Because God is ALL powerful, He can do _____ things.

9. Because God is TRUSTworthy, I can always _____ Him.

10. Because God is FAITHful, I have _____ in Him.

11. Because God is the ONE true God, He is number _____ to me.

12. Because God is AWEsome, I stand in _____ of Him.

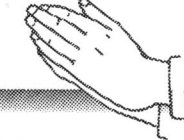

Comparing Our Fathers
Game

For this reason I kneel before the Father, from whom his whole family in heaven and on earth derives its name. (Ephesians 3:14–15)

This critical thinking game encourages the children to focus on the similarities and differences between their earthly and heavenly fathers. Make three columns on a bulletin board or on a white sheet of posterboard. Label each column with one of the following: OUR DAD; OUR FATHER, GOD; BOTH.

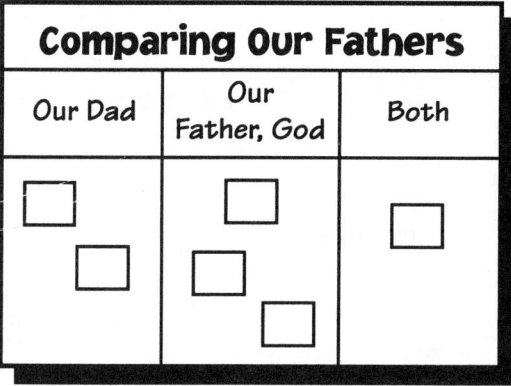

Cut out the cards below and turn them facedown. One child selects a card for you to read. The children must then decide if what the card says is true of dads, God, the Father, or both dads and God. Pin the card to the correct column. (If using posterboard, put a check mark in the proper column.) Answers are as follows: 1. D; 2. B; 3. D; 4. D; 5. G; 6. B; 7. G; 8. B; 9. G; 10. G; 11. G; 12. D; 13. G; 14. D; 15. B; 16. G.

1. He may not be around when I need him.	2. He loves me because I belong to him.	3. He sometimes makes mistakes.	4. He sometimes gets mad when I do something wrong.
5. He is always with me wherever I go, even though I can't see Him.	6. He does not like the bad things I do but always loves me.	7. He always has time to listen to everything I say.	8. He thinks I am very special.
9. He never does anything wrong.	10. He always knows the right thing to do.	11. He sees everything I do.	12. He gives me hugs.
13. He is in charge of the whole world.	14. Sometimes he sleeps, and I'm not supposed to wake him.	15. He wants to give me good things.	16. He is making a home where I can live with Him forever.

© Shining Star Publications

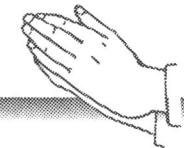

"God's Good Gifts" Can

Craft

... from generation to generation we will recount your praise. (Psalm 79:13)

Everyone benefits from remembering God's goodness and celebrating His answers to prayer. The craft described below is fun for the children to make for their families and will help them remember the many blessings God gives all of us and the way He has answered our prayers. (These make wonderful Christmas gifts.)

Materials Needed (per child):
any type of clean can with a lid, gift wrap, ribbon or lace, glue, one construction paper square containing the words "God's Good Gifts", one copy of the letter below

Directions:
1. Have the children cut and glue wrapping paper to fit around their cans.
2. The children can glue one of the construction paper squares to their cans.
3. Let the children glue lace or ribbon around the top and bottom of their cans if they want.
4. They could also glue a bow on the lids to make the cans look like gifts.
5. Send home the note below explaining the purpose of the can.

Dear Family,

　　This can is a perfect way for us to remember the many gifts God gives us. We can write down special ways God blesses us throughout the year and ways He answers our prayers on pieces of paper and put them in the can. On different days, perhaps Thanksgiving or Christmas, we can pull out the papers and read them together to remind us of God's gifts to us.

© Shining Star Publications

SS48832

Prayer Calendar
Bulletin Board

. . . in the morning my prayer comes before you. (Psalm 88:13)

This is a wonderful way to help children learn about all the people and things they can pray for.

Materials Needed:
border of your choice, thirty-eight 3" x 5" cards, markers, yardstick

Directions:
Number the days of the month on the cards (from 1 to 28–31). On the other cards, write the days of the week. Use the yardstick to measure seven even columns on the bulletin board. Place the day cards at the top of these columns.

Turn over the numbered cards. Write one item to pray for each day, as listed below. Arrange these on the board, number side out, starting card #1 on the appropriate day of the week for the current month.

On the first day of the month, turn over card #1 and pin it to the board, with the prayer side showing. Ask the children to pray for the person or need listed on the card. Suggest specific things the children could ask God for.

1. Thank God for making you just as you are.
2. Pray for your mother.
3. Pray for your father.
4. Pray for your brother(s).
5. Pray for your sister(s).
6. Pray for your pet(s).
7. Ask God to help you obey your parents.
8. Thank God for your family.
9. Pray for your grandmas.
10. Pray for your grandpas.
11. Pray for your uncles.
12. Pray for your aunts.
13. Pray for your cousins.
14. Ask God to help you be kind.
15. Thank God for your school.
16. Pray for your best friend.
17. Pray for all the friends you can think of.
18. Pray for your teacher.
19. Pray for the pastor of your church.
20. Pray for your Sunday school teacher.
21. Ask God to help you be a good learner.
22. Thank God for your country.
23. Pray for your babysitter(s).
24. Pray for the U.S. president.
25. Pray for your state's governor.
26. Pray for children who don't know Jesus.
27. Pray for missionaries.
28. Pray for Christians in other countries.
29. Pray for people who don't have Bibles.
30. Pray for homeless people.
31. Ask God to help you grow up and become what He wants you to be.

Alphabetical Order Praise Cards

Every day I will praise you and extol your name for ever and ever. (Psalm 145:2)

This game helps the children learn a wonderful variety of characteristics that describe God. It is also a great way to reinforce beginning letter sounds and letter recognition.

Cut apart the cards below. Read them to the children and let them tell you the beginning sound. They can help each other put them in alphabetical order on a piece of posterboard or other work space. Or, let groups of children work together to read the cards and arrange them in alphabetical order.

Awesome	**J**ust	**S**trong
Big	**K**ind	**T**rue
Caring	**L**ove	**U**nchanging
Does what He says	**M**ost High	**V**ery holy
Eternal	**N**ever wrong	**W**ise
Faithful	**O**ne and only God	E**X**cellent
Good	**P**atient	**Y**ours and mine
Here	**Q**uiet	**Z**ealous to save us
In charge	**R**ight	

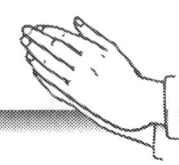

Loving and Praising God

Songs

With praise and thanksgiving they sang to the Lord: "He is good; his love to Israel endures forever." And all the people gave a great shout of praise to the Lord . . . (Ezra 3:11)

The song below is fun for the children to sing and dance to. It will remind them of who they love and praise.

(Tune: "Ezekiel Saw Dem Dry Bones")

> I love, I love, I love <u>God.</u>
> I love, I love, I love <u>God.</u>
> I love, I love, I love <u>God.</u>
> Now praise the name of the Lord.
> (Shout): PRAISE THE LORD!

(You could also substitute the names of the children for the word "God.")

> Examples: I love, I love, I love Amber.
> I love, I love, I love Leah.
> I love, I love, I love Ben.
> Now praise the name of the Lord.
> (Shout): PRAISE THE LORD!

> 2nd verse: I praise, I praise, I praise God.
> I praise, I praise, I praise God.
> I praise, I praise, I praise God.
> Now praise the name of the Lord.
> (Shout): PRAISE THE LORD!

The song below reminds children to praise and serve the Lord day and night. For engaging fun, teach the children how to clap to the beat.

(Tune: "Hot Cross Buns")

Praise the Lord. Praise the Lord.
In the morning, in the evening,
Praise the Lord.

Love the Lord. Love the Lord.
In the morning, in the evening,
Love the Lord.

God is good. God is good.
In the morning, in the evening,
God is good.

I will pray. I will pray.
In the morning, in the evening,
I will pray.

Serve the Lord. Serve the Lord.
In the morning, in the evening,
Serve the Lord.

Thank the Lord. Thank the Lord.
In the morning, in the evening,
Thank the Lord.

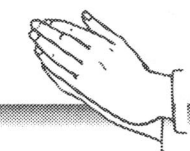

Kitchen Orchestra

David and all the Israelites were celebrating with all their might before God, with songs and with harps, lyres, tambourines, cymbals and trumpets. (1 Chronicles 13:8)

Let the children help make the instruments below that they can use to sing the songs on pages 21–22.

Materials Needed:

a variety of the following: cardboard tubes (from toilet paper or paper towels), wax paper, rubber bands, shoeboxes or other sturdy boxes, oatmeal boxes with lids, salt containers, film canisters, wooden spoons or dowels, rice or beans, coffee cans with lids, heavy disposable plastic plates, jingle bells, clothespins, pipe cleaners, pint jars, water, plastic spoons or tongue depressors, paper or plastic cups, aluminum pie plates, elastic, bowls or pans

Brass Instruments

cardboard tubes with a circle of wax paper secured over the end with a rubber band; Child hums into the tube.

String Instruments

Stretch rubber bands over a shallow, sturdy box that is open on top. (A greeting card box with the bottom inside the top works great.) Pluck with fingers.

Percussion Instruments

(These seem to be the favorites of all children!)

Drum—empty oatmeal box with lid glued on, coffee cans with plastic lids, or overturned bowls or pans; Pound with hands, rubber spatulas, or wooden spoons.

Shakers—film canisters containing a few grains of rice or beans with the lids glued on; Shake.

Sticks—two wooden spoons or dowels that can be clanked against each other

Cymbals—aluminum pie plates or plastic disposable plates; Punch two holes in the center of each. Thread an elastic strip through them and tie it. Slip a hand under the loop of elastic on each plate and bang together.

Bongos—two salt boxes taped together; Pound with hands.

Tambourine—heavy disposable plate (plastic) with holes punched and jingle bells attached; Shake.

Marimba—pint jars filled with different amounts of water; Hit them on their sides with a spoon or tongue depressor.

Bells—jingle bells attached around the top of a clothespin (not the spring-action kind) with a pipe cleaner; Shake.

Clappers—disposable paper or plastic cups placed upside down on a table; Clap them up and down against the tabletop.

Sing Praise to God
Songs

Sing to the Lord, you saints of his; praise his holy name. (Psalm 30:4)
Below and on page 22 are some simple praise songs the children can sing to familiar tunes.

Thank You, Jesus
(Tune: "Are You Sleeping?")

This song can be sung with the children echoing you.

Thank You, Jesus. Thank You, Jesus.
Praise Your name. Praise Your name.
You alone are worthy. You alone are worthy.
Praise Your name. Praise Your name.

Praise the Lord
(Tune: "Row, Row, Row Your Boat")

Praise, praise, praise the Lord.
Praise the Lord above.
Thank You. Thank You. Thank You. Thank You,
For Your gift of love.

Praise and Glory
(Tune: "Happy Birthday to You")

Praise and glory to You.
Praise and glory to You.
Praise to Father, Son, and Spirit;
Praise and glory to You.

The Lord Above
(Tune: chorus of "Jingle Bells")

Praise the Lord; Praise the Lord;
Praise the Lord above.
He is holy, He is true,
And He wraps me in His love.

Sing Praise to God continued
Songs

Praise the Lord, for the Lord is good; sing praise to his name, for that is pleasant. (Psalm 135:3)

Glory Be to God
(Tune: "This Old Man")

Praise the Lord. Praise the Lord.
Hallelujah; praise the Lord.
As we sing and clap and give Him all our praise,
Glory be to God always.

Praise the Lord. Praise the Lord.
Hallelujah; praise the Lord.
With a toot-toot, strum-strum, jingle-jangle song,
Praise the Lord the whole day long.

Praise Forever
(Tune: "Skip to My Lou")

Praise, praise, praise to my Lord.
Praise, praise, praise to my Lord.
Praise, praise, praise to my Lord.
Praise to my Lord forever.

Hallelujah
(Tune: "Found a Peanut")

Hallelujah. Hallelujah. Hallelujah. Amen.
Hallelujah. Hallelujah. Hallelujah. Amen.

Praise and glory. Praise and glory. Praise and glory. Hallelu.
Hallelujah. Praise and glory. Praise and glory. Hallelu.

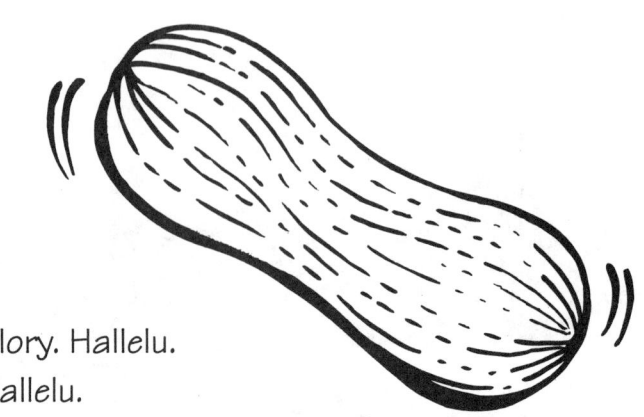

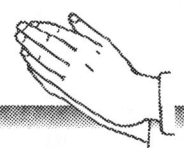

Magical Musical Sounds
Finger Play

Let everything that has breath praise the Lord . . . (Psalm 150:6)

Read Psalm 150 to the children. Then let them make their own joyful noise unto the Lord with the finger play below.

Praise the Lord. Praise the Lord.	*(Clap hands in rhythm.)*
Praise Him with the trumpet. TOOT, TOOT, TOOT	*(Hold hands, one in front of the other, up to mouth.)*
Praise Him with the harp. STRUM, STRUM, STRUM	*(Move hands as if playing a harp.)*
Praise Him with the tambourine. JINGLE, JINGLE, JINGLE	*(Clap the fist of one hand against the open palm of other.)*
Praise Him with the flute. HOOT, HOOT, HOOT	*(Hold hands to side of mouth.)*
Praise Him with the cymbals. CLASH, CLASH, CLASH	*(Slap hands together with big motions.)*
Praise the Lord. Yes, praise the Lord.	*(Clap hands.)*

God's Will for Us

Be joyful always; pray continually; give thanks in all circumstances, for this is God's will for you in Christ Jesus. (1 Thessalonians 5:16–18)

The Bible commands us to have joy, to pray continually, and to give thanks for every circumstance. God wants us to do these things. The children will remember these commands by singing them.

(Tune: chorus of "Jesus Loves Me")

Be joyful always. Be joyful always. Be joyful always.
This is God's will for you.

Pray without stopping. Pray without stopping. Pray without stopping.
This is God's will for you.

Give thanks in all things. Give thanks in all things. Give thanks in all things.
This is God's will for you.

© Shining Star Publications

Thanksgiving Place Mat

Let us come before him with thanksgiving . . . (Psalm 95:2)

Have your children make their very own thanksgiving place mats following the directions below.

Materials Needed:
an 11" x 14" sheet of construction paper and a copy of the pictures below per child, clear and colored adhesive-backed paper, scissors, glue, crayons

Directions:
Have the children color and cut out any pictures below of things they are thankful for. They can glue them to the 11" x 14" sheets of construction paper. Let them add any other pictures they want. Cut each child a sheet of clear adhesive-backed paper slightly larger than his or her picture. Remove the backing. Place the picture facedown on the adhesive. Then add colored adhesive-backed paper to the back of the picture. Trim the edges.

© Shining Star Publications

SS48832

"Express Your Emotions" Book

... "In my distress I called to the Lord, and he answered me ..." (Jonah 2:1)

God wants to know when you are happy, sad, mad, or scared. Pray to Him to tell Him what you are feeling.

Cut out the boxes below. Draw a picture in each one. Make a cover for your book. Staple or tie the pages together with yarn.

I am happy when . . .	**I am sad when . . .**
Thank You, God!	**Please help me not to be sad, Lord!**
I get scared when . . .	**I am mad when . . .**
Please help me not to be scared, Lord!	**Please help me not to be mad, Lord!**

I'm Wonderfully Made

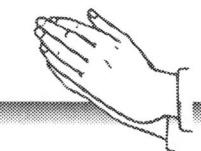

I praise you because I am fearfully and wonderfully made . . . (Psalm 139:14)

Teach the children the song below they can sing to learn how magnificently God made each of them!

(Tune: "Mary Had a Little Lamb")

I praise You because I am
Wonderful, wonderful.
I praise You because I am
So wonderfully made.

Thank You for my <u>nose and toes</u>,
<u>Nose and toes</u>, <u>nose and toes</u>.
Thank You for my <u>nose and toes</u>—
I'm wonderfully made.

(Point with both hands to each body part as it is named.)

Substitute the following where underlined:

hips and lips
wrists and fists
eyes and thighs
chin and shins

After singing the song, spread out a large sheet of butcher paper. Have each child draw or cut out a picture showing a body part he or she is thankful for. Let the children take turns telling what body part they are thankful for and why (examples—legs for running races; eyes for seeing beautiful flowers).

You could also give each child a picture of a person and have the children circle each of the five senses. Then they could draw pictures showing how they use their five senses to enjoy God's creation.

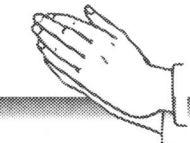

Pray Banner

. . . pray for each other . . . (James 5:16)

Be sure to let the children know that they need to remember others in their prayers. Then let them make a "pray banner" to help remind them to pray for others.

Materials Needed (per child):
copy of the letters and square on this page, 5 pieces of posterboard cut into 4" x 4" squares, yarn or ribbon, scissors, glue, hole punch, crayons

Directions:
1. Give each child a copy of the letters and square.
2. Have the children color and cut out their copies.
3. The children should glue the letters and square to the posterboard pieces.
4. Help the children punch holes in all four corners of the squares, except the last square. In this square, only punch two holes, one in each top corner.
5. Help the children use pieces of yarn or ribbon to tie the squares together and to tie a piece at the top for hanging.

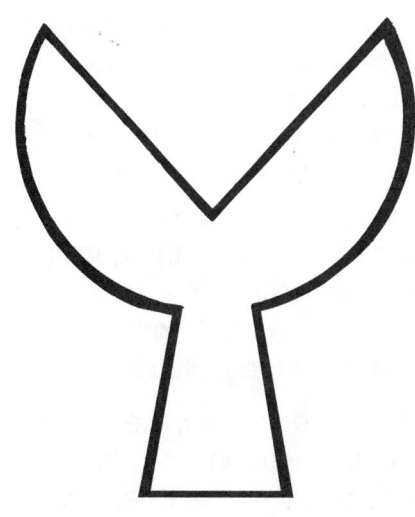

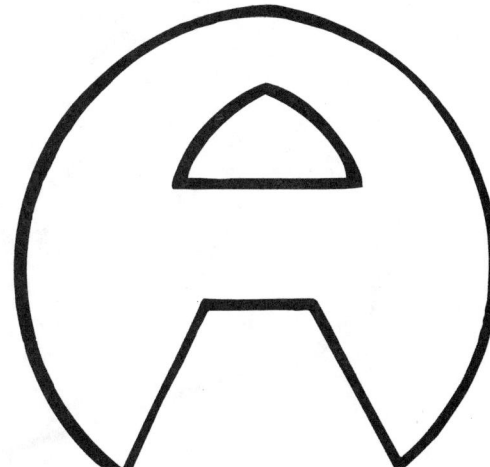

Special Things to Pray for

Bulletin Board and Activity

But the fruit of the Spirit is love, joy, peace, patience, kindness, goodness, faithfulness, gentleness and self-control . . . (Galatians 5:22–23)

This bulletin board and corresponding activity provide a nice variety of Christian ideals the children should pray for.

Materials Needed:
nine colors of posterboard
one copy of page 29 per child
scissors

Directions:

1. Cut nine big hearts out of nine different colors of posterboard. Write one of the following on each heart: *Love, Joy, Peace, Patience, Kindness, Goodness, Faithfulness, Gentleness, Self-Control*. Attach these to the bulletin board.

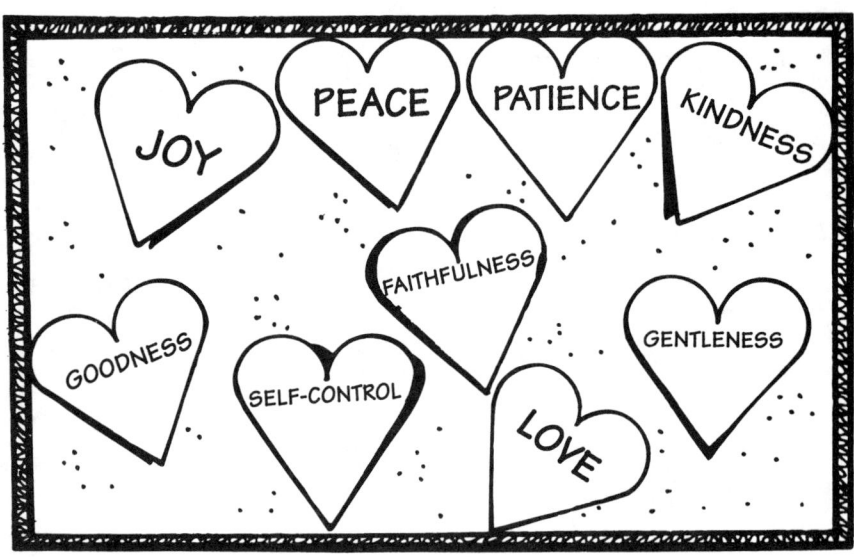

2. Give each child a copy of page 29.

3. Focus on one heart word per day. Discuss the daily word and ask the children how it might show up in their actions and responses. Help the children fill in the letters for the featured value.

4. Lead the children in praying for God to help them have that quality in their hearts and to show it in their actions that day.

5. Throughout the day, let the children color the featured heart on their pages when each of them experiences that quality. At this time, you should also write the child's name on the big heart containing the name of the quality that you attached to the board. You could also write a brief note describing what the child did.

At the end of class each day, pray with the children, thanking God for helping them have that quality in their hearts.

© Shining Star Publications

Special Things to Pray for

Egg Request
Game

"As for me, far be it from me that I should sin against the Lord by failing to pray for you. And I will teach you the way that is good and right." (1 Samuel 12:23)

This game is fun for the children to do in class or at home.

Materials Needed (per child or group):
12 plastic eggs, egg carton, copy of the cards below

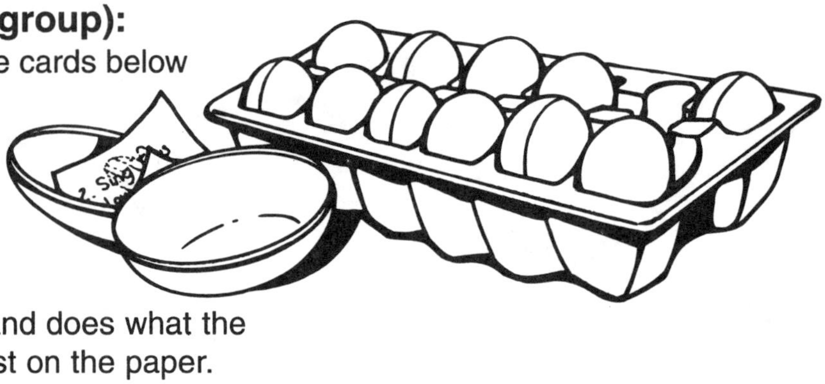

Directions:
1. Cut out the cards.
2. Put one in each egg.
3. Put the eggs in the egg carton.
4. A child selects an egg, opens it, and does what the paper says or prays for the request on the paper.

---

1. Pray for someone in the room.

2. Sing "Jesus Loves Me."

3. Thank God for something.

4. Ask God to bless someone you love.

5. Thank God for loving you.

6. Clap and say, "Praise the Lord."

7. Thank God for always being with you.

8. Pray for your best friend.

9. Thank God for the Bible.

10. Say, "I love Jesus because He first loved me."

11. Hug someone and tell this person, "God loves you and so do I."

12. Repeat this Bible verse: *Give thanks to the Lord, for he is good . . .* (Psalm 118:1)

A Gift of Love

Color the frame below. Cut it out. Glue it to construction paper. Draw or attach a photo of someone special in the middle—your mom or dad, grandma or grandpa, or neighbor. Give it as a gift.

...we pray for you because we have heard of your faith in Christ Jesus... (Colossians 1:3,4)

Prayer Puzzle

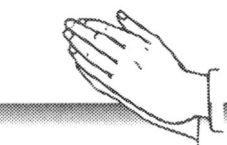

God wants us to pray for everyone—even people we might not want to pray for. Praying to God is like talking on the telephone. We cannot see the person we are speaking to, but we know he or she is there listening to us. Even though we cannot see God, we know He always hears us when we talk to Him.

Use the code numbers on the telephone pad to learn about some people the Bible says we should pray for.

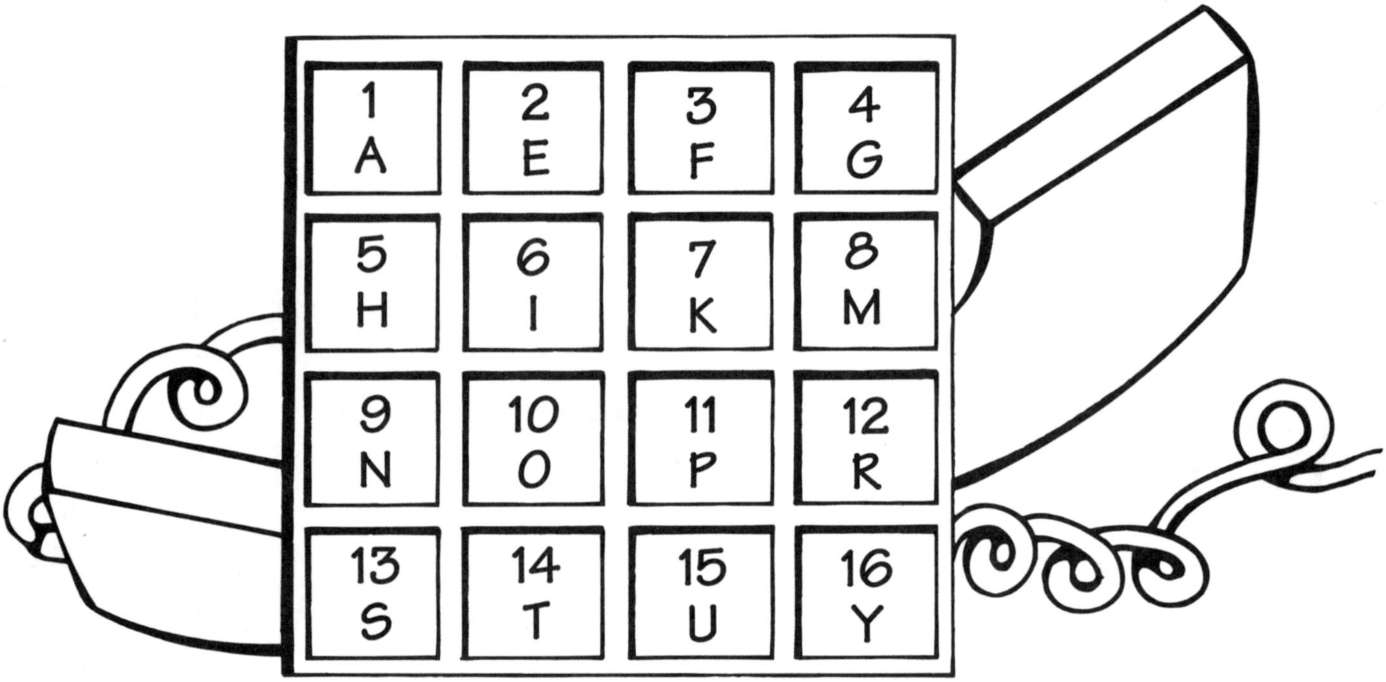

"... P R A Y   F O R
    11 12 1 16   3 10 12

T H O S E   W H O
14 5 10 13 2   5 10

M I S T R E A T
8 6 13 14 12 2 1 14

Y O U." (Luke 6:28)
16 10 15

Pray Throughout the Day
Action Story

Seven times a day I praise you . . . (Psalm 119:164)

The interactive story below and on page 34 helps the children understand that we can pray anytime during the day. The children will love doing the motions for Jesse (see italics) and you can use a teaching clock. If you don't have one, make one using the patterns on page 34. As you tell this story, show the times mentioned.

Jesse was a happy little boy who loved Jesus very much. One day, he learned this Bible verse, *Seven times a day I praise you . . .* So Jesse decided to have seven prayer times every day.

At <u>8:00</u> in the morning, Jesse's mother said, "Time to wake up, Jesse." Jesse sat up in bed, *stretched his arms over his head* and then *bowed his head* to pray. "Thank You, Lord, for this new day. Help me as I work and play. In Jesus' name, Amen*."

Before *Jesse ate his breakfast, he bowed his head* and prayed, "Thank You for our daily food. You are kind and You are good. In Jesus' name, Amen*."

After breakfast, *Jesse brushed his teeth, combed his hair,* and did his chores. At <u>10:00</u>, he *built a tower* out of blocks and *played the piano* for a while. At <u>noon</u>, his mother said, "Lunch is ready." Jesse *washed his hands* and remembered to *bow his head* and thank God before eating. "Thank You for our daily food. You are kind and You are good. In Jesus' name, Amen*."

Jesse's mother read him a story before his nap time at <u>2:00</u>. Jesse *laid his head* on the pillow, *closed his eyes,* and quietly sang a praise song to God.** Soon Jesse was fast asleep.

At <u>4:00</u>, Jesse woke up suddenly. He *yawned*. Then he thought this prayer: "Thank You, God, for loving me. Thank You for my family. In Jesus' name, Amen*." He *put on his jacket and hat and boots and gloves* and went outside to play.

Jesse played until his dad came home at <u>6:00</u>. Then he went into the house, *took off his gloves, boots, hat, and jacket.* "Dinner's ready," his mother called. Jesse and his dad *washed their hands.* Jesse *bowed his head* and prayed in his mind while his daddy thanked God for dinner.

Pray Throughout... continued

Action Story

After dinner, Jesse and his dad *threw* a ball to each other and did *arm exercises* together. Soon it was 8:00 and time for Jesse to go to bed.

Jesse remembered to *wash his face* and *brush his teeth*. He also remembered to *kneel* beside his bed and talk to God one more time. "Thank You for this wonderful day. I'm sorry I did some wrong things like wanting my own way. Help me always to obey. In Jesus' name, Amen*."

Then Jesse's mom and dad *hugged* him and helped him into bed. He *tucked the quilt under his chin, closed his eyes,* and went to sleep, happy that he had kept his goal of praying seven times that day.

*Instead of this ending, the children could sing the prayer ending as given on page 8.
**Choose a praise song from pages 21–22.

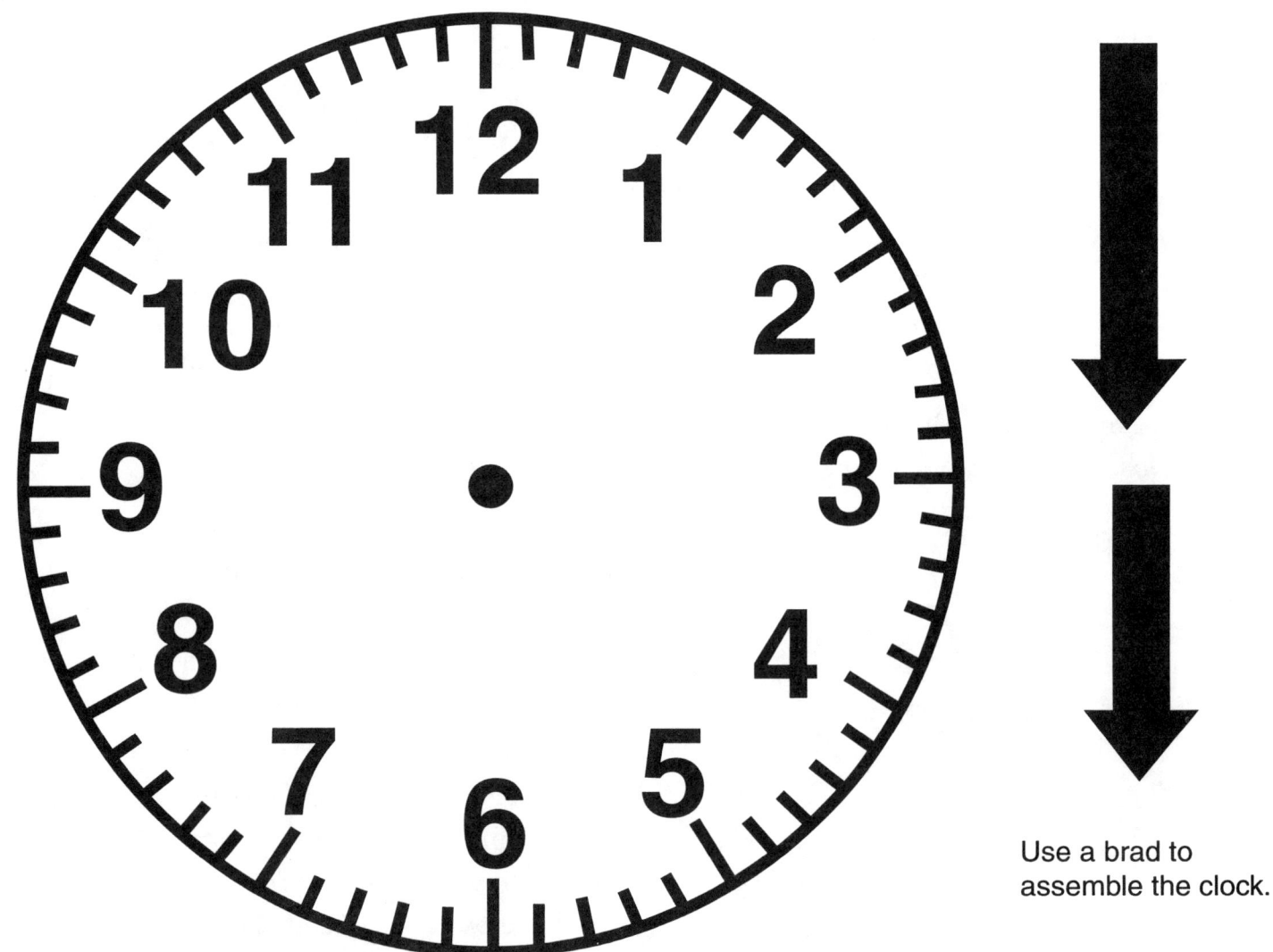

Use a brad to assemble the clock.

Prayer Grid
Game

I urge, then, first of all, that requests, prayers, intercession and thanksgiving be made for everyone—for kings and all those in authority . . . (1 Timothy 2:1–2)

This game can be played to help children remember to pray for a wonderful variety of people. Feel free to change the names on the card. You can include the children's names, teachers' names, people in different towns, states, countries, etc.

Materials Needed:
16 identical chips, bottle caps, cards, etc.; one copy of the grid below; a container in which to store the 16 pieces

Directions:
1. Enlarge the grid. On each square of the grid, write a person in authority to pray for. Some suggestions include these: President of the U.S., Vice President, governor, senators, state representatives, judges, school principal, teachers, minister, fathers, mothers, grandparents, baby sitters, police officers, doctors.

2. On the chips, bottle caps, or cards, write the coordinates as follows: P1, P2, P3, P4, R1, R2, R3, R4, A1, A2, A3, A4, Y1, Y2, Y3, Y4.

3. Put all the pieces in a container. Children can take turns drawing a piece, reading the coordinates, and locating the correct square. The children can then pray for the person listed in that square.

	P	R	A	Y
1				
2				
3				
4				

Praying People Puzzles

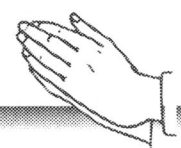

Do not be anxious about anything, but in everything, by prayer and petition, with thanksgiving, present your requests to God. (Philippians 4:6)

These puzzles are fun for the children to complete to learn about people in the Bible who prayed and what they prayed for.

Materials Needed:
one copy of this page, posterboard, glue, scissors, crayons

Directions:
Glue this page to posterboard. Color the pictures. Cut out the shapes and cut along the puzzle lines. Have the children match each Bible person with what he or she asked God for. The puzzle pieces can also be pinned to a bulletin board, and the children can match them and pin them in place.

- King Hezekiah — Healing
- Hannah — A Son
- Jonah — Deliverance
- Elijah — Rain
- Moses — His Brother and Sister
- David — His Problems
- Job — His Friends
- Abraham — A City
- Nehemiah — His Nation, Israel
- Solomon — Wisdom

© Shining Star Publications

Lots of People Prayed

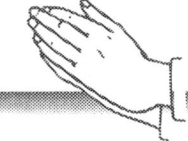

1 Samuel 1:11, 1 Samuel 16:23, Daniel 6:10, Acts 16:25, Mark 14:38

Sing joyfully to the Lord . . . (Psalm 33:1)

The song below is a great way to teach the children about people who prayed. Read the Bible stories listed above to the children and discuss each one with them.

(Tune: "She'll Be Comin' 'Round the Mountain")

Hannah prayed the Lord would give to her a son.
Hannah prayed the Lord would give to her a son.
    Glory. Hallelujah. Praises.
    Glory. Hallelujah. Praises.
Hannah prayed the Lord would give to her a son.

David played his harp and sang unto the Lord.
David played his harp and sang unto the Lord.
    Glory. Hallelujah. Praises.
    Glory. Hallelujah. Praises.
David played his harp and sang unto the Lord.

Daniel prayed unto the Lord three times a day.
Daniel prayed unto the Lord three times a day.
    Glory. Hallelujah. Praises.
    Glory. Hallelujah. Praises.
Daniel prayed unto the Lord three times a day.

Paul and Silas prayed and sang to God in jail.
Paul and Silas prayed and sang to God in jail.
    Glory. Hallelujah. Praises.
    Glory. Hallelujah. Praises.
Paul and Silas prayed and sang to God in jail.

Jesus tells His children all to watch and pray.
Jesus tells His children all to watch and pray.
    Glory. Hallelujah. Praises.
    Glory. Hallelujah. Praises.
Jesus tells His children all to watch and pray.

© Shining Star Publications

Daniel Prayed No Matter What!

Based on Daniel 6

. . . he went home to his upstairs room where the windows opened toward Jerusalem. Three times a day he got down on his knees and prayed, giving thanks to his God . . . (Daniel 6:10)

Color the picture. Glue it to heavy paper. When dry, cut on the puzzle lines. Work the puzzle or let a friend work it.

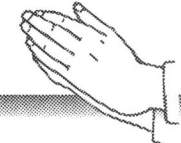

Be Like Daniel
Based on Daniel 6

. . . And when Daniel was lifted from the den, no wound was found on him, because he had trusted in his God. (Daniel 6:23)

This song emphasizes the faith Daniel had and encourages the children to be good like Daniel. Have two children form a drawbridge by standing, facing each other, with hands raised, clasped together. The rest of the children form a circle and pass under the clasped hands. On the last line of each stanza, the "bridge" comes down and catches a "Daniel." (In this game, explain to the children that they are caught being good—being like Daniel.) The caught "Daniel" sits out until everyone is caught. The last two children caught become the next drawbridge.

(Tune: "London Bridge")

In the morning, Daniel prayed. Daniel prayed. Daniel prayed.
In the morning, Daniel prayed.
Be like Daniel.

In the noontime, Daniel prayed. Daniel prayed. Daniel prayed.
In the noontime, Daniel prayed.
Be like Daniel.

In the evening, Daniel prayed. Daniel prayed. Daniel prayed.
In the evening, Daniel prayed.
Be like Daniel.

Daniel trusted in his God, in his God, in his God.
Daniel trusted in his God.
Be like Daniel.

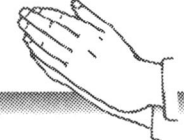

Happy or Sad?
Based on Daniel 6

. . . may they be happy and joyful. (Psalm 68:3)

Use a medium-point pen or felt-tipped marker to draw a simple happy face (two eyes and a smile inside a circle) on the right palm of each child. Draw a similar sad face on the other palm. Draw the faces so the children can see them (not upside down). Tell the children to listen to the story and do what you say. Note: Feel free to add any information or questions to the story.

- Daniel was a man who loved God. (Is this a happy thing or a sad thing? Show me your hand with the happy face.)

- Some people who didn't love God hated Daniel. (Is this happy or sad? Show me your hand with the sad face.)

- Daniel prayed three times every day. Daniel loved God. (Did this make God happy? Show me your hand that gives the answer.)

- The people who didn't love God said Daniel had to stop praying. (How do you think Daniel felt?)

- Daniel prayed to God anyhow. (How do you think God felt?)

- The bad people said Daniel had to be thrown into the den of hungry lions. (How do you think Daniel felt?)

- The king liked Daniel. He didn't like it when Daniel was put in with the lions. (How do you think the king felt?)

- The lions didn't hurt Daniel because God had shut the lions' mouths. (How do you think Daniel felt?)

- The king was glad Daniel was safe. (How do you think he felt when he saw Daniel was OK?)

© Shining Star Publications

SS48832

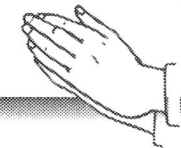

Wanna-Be Song
Psalm 108, Daniel 6, Jonah 1, Acts 2:14

The lips of the wise spread knowledge . . . (Proverbs 15:7)

Children always "wanna-be" things when they grow up. As they learn this song, they just might want to be like the Bible people featured in it!

(Tune: "If You're Happy and You Know It")

If you wanna be like David, learn to sing. (Pretend to
If you wanna be like David, learn to sing. strum a harp
    David learned to sing a song, or guitar.)
    Praising God the whole day long.
If you wanna be like David, learn to sing.

If you wanna be like Daniel, learn to pray. (Fold hands,
If you wanna be like Daniel, learn to pray. as if praying.)
    Daniel prayed three times a day,
    And the lions stayed away.
If you wanna be like Daniel, learn to pray.

If you wanna be like Jonah, learn to swim. (Make big arm
If you wanna be like Jonah, learn to swim. movements,
    Jonah tried to run away as if swimming.)
    'Til he learned he must obey.
If you wanna be like Jonah, learn to swim.

If you wanna be like Peter, learn to preach. (Wave one hand
If you wanna be like Peter, learn to preach. in the air with
    Peter learned to preach God's Word, finger pointed.)
    Giving glory to the Lord.
If you wanna be like Peter, learn to preach.

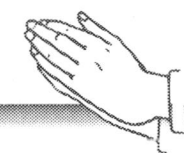

Any Place, Any Time

pray continually (1 Thessalonians 5:17)

It is important to remember that we can talk to God any place at any time. God always likes to hear from us.

Color the pictures of places where you can pray.

Pray and Be Happy!

A happy heart makes the face cheerful... (Proverbs 15:13)

When you pray to God, you are happy and God is happy. When you are happy, you smile.

Connect the dots from A to Z. Color the picture.

Prayer Fun
Action Verses

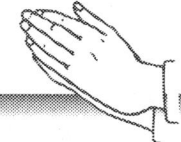

Teach the children the Bible verses and actions below that they can do to remind them to pray every day.

Sing (Cup hands around mouth.)
to the Lord, (Extend arms over head, hands open.)
all the earth . . . (Make a circle with arms, meeting hands with a clap.)
(1 Chronicles 16:23)

I will praise you, (Clap hands a few times.)
O Lord, (Extend arms over head, hands open.)
with all my heart . . . (Cross hands over heart.)
(Psalm 138:1)

Those who know (Touch fingertips of both hands to forehead.)
your name (Extend arms over head, hands open.)
will trust in you . . . (Hug self.)
(Psalm 9:10)

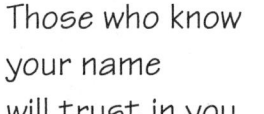

The Lord (Extend arms over head, hands open.)
is near (Cross hands over heart.)
to all (Extend arms out to the sides.)
who call on him . . . (Fold hands like praying.)
(Psalm 145:18)

Special Cards

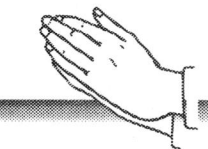

. . . encourage one another and build each other up, just as in fact you are doing. (1 Thessalonians 5:11)

Ask the children to think of someone they might need to pray for—perhaps someone who is sick or lonely. Then let them create wonderful greeting cards they can give away.

Materials Needed:
5" x 7" sheets of card stock, folded in half; pencils; markers; scissors

Directions:
1. On the folded cards, trace around one of each child's hands with the pinky finger on the fold. Keep each child's fingers together so that the outline will look like praying hands.
2. Cut these out for the children, being careful not to cut too much of the fold away.
3. Write on the board, *I am praying for you.* Have the children copy this inside their cards and sign their names. Then let the children draw fingernails, rings, bracelets, etc., on the outside of their cards.

Prayer Pendants
The children can wear these pendants to remind them and others to pray!

Materials Needed (per child):
copy of the pendant to the left on heavy paper, yarn, crayons, scissors, glue

Directions:
1. Have the children color and cut out their pendants.
2. The children should fold their pendants on the dotted lines.
3. Help the children glue a long piece of yarn on the fold.
4. Tell the children to glue the pendant halves together and tie the yarn to make necklaces.

© Shining Star Publications

Let's Go Pray!

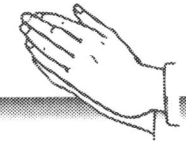

..."*Let us go to the house of the Lord.*" (Psalm 122:1)

The children below want to go to church to pray. Help them find the church.

Rhyme Time

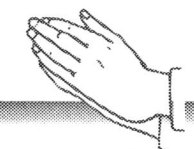

. . . they were holding golden bowls full of incense, which are the prayers of the saints. (Revelation 5:8)

Teach the children the simple prayers below they can say at church, school, home, or anywhere!

Thank You for loving me.
Thank You for salvation free.
Thank You for my family.
Thank You for making me ME.

Lord, You keep me safe from fear,
And You wipe away each tear.
You put me in my family dear.
You fill me up with joy and cheer.
Lord, I know You're always near.
Yes, I know that You're right here.

Thank You for this brand new day.
Give me loving words to say.
Keep me safe at work and play.
Show me how to live Your way.

Thank You for good food to eat—
Both the sour and the sweet.
Thank You for the clothes I wear
And the toys I learn to share.
Thank You for my parents, too.
But most of all—thank You for YOU.

You are kind and good and true.
You see everything I do.
Every day, Your love is new.
I'm glad I belong to You.

Help me grow with all my might.
Help me know You day and night.
Help me show others You are right.
Help me glow with Your true light.

© Shining Star Publications

Sssh! Prayer in Progress
Door Hanger

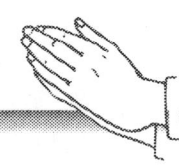

The door hanger below is perfect for children to make to hang on their doors when they want some quiet time with God.

Materials Needed (per child):

copy of the door hanger below on heavy paper, crayons, scissors, glue

Directions:

1. Have each child color and cut out a door hanger.
2. Show the children how to fold their hangers in half and glue the sides together.
3. Each child can hang the hanger on a door at home when he or she wants to be alone in prayer.

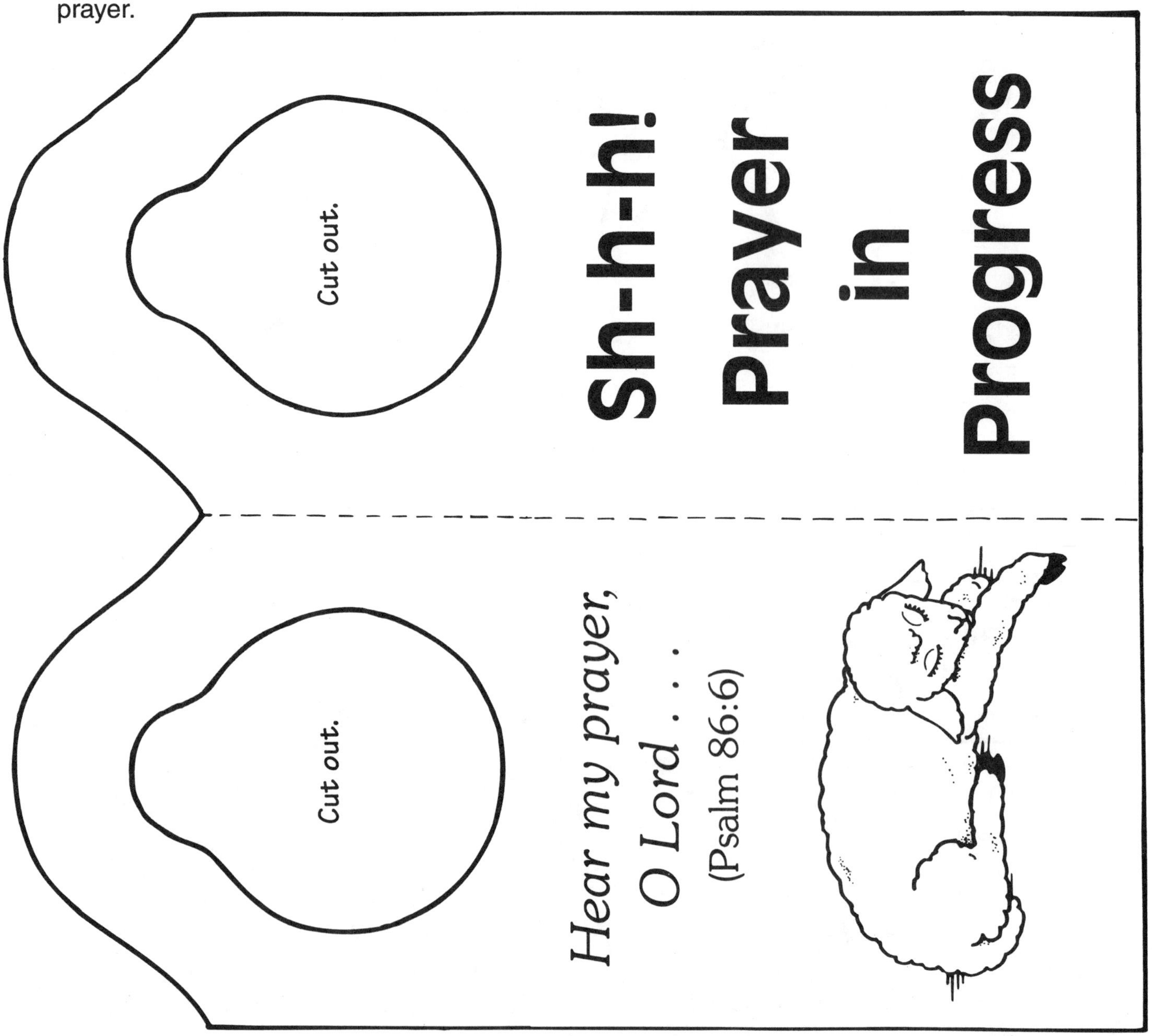

Sh-h-h! Prayer in Progress

Hear my prayer, O Lord . . . . (Psalm 86:6)

Cut out.

© Shining Star Publications

48

SS48832